MRS. SCHRÖDINGER'S BREAST

Poems

Quinton Hallett

First U.S. edition 2015

Editor and Publisher: Laura LeHew

Proofreaders: Judith H. Montgomery
                Nancy Carol Moody

Cover: 200704 Oil on Panel 48" x 60"
         © 2007 Dennis A. Gould
         Quinton Hallett Collection

Copyright © 2015 Quinton Hallett

www.utteredchaos.org

All Rights Reserved. Except for brief passages quoted in a newspaper, magazine, radio or television review, no portion of this book may be reproduced in any form or by any means, electronic or mechanical, including photocopying and recording, or by any information storage and retrieval system, without written permission from the Publisher. All rights to the works printed herein remain with the author.

ISBN: 978-0-9889366-4-5

for D

CONTENTS

ENTANGLEMENT

Self-Portrait as Bruise   1
Deadlock   2
Square Roots   4
At Salt Creek Falls   6
Mrs. Schrödinger Ties Her Own Flies   7

DOUBLE-SLIT THEORY

Self-Portrait as Insomnia   11
Freeze Tag   12
M & Ms   14
Self-Portrait as Quarrel   16
Défense de Fumer   17
When a Mermaid Comes Undone   18
Dinner at the *Déjà Vu*   20
How to Make a Voodoo Doll   21
Worry People   22

DECOHERENCE

Mrs. Schrödinger's Mirage of Convenience   27
Self-Portrait as Roots   28
Belonging   29
Particle or Wave   30
One does not tell the future   it tells us   31
How the Temporary Becomes Permanent   32
What Does Not Require Wings   33
Mirage   34
Scant Measure   35
Seventh Side of the Die   36
Instructions for a First-Time Widow   37
Her Treasured Extravagance   38

FIELD THEORY

When Demons Blink   41
On the Verge   42
Anny's Conundrum   43
My Avocado, This Cheeky Addiction   44
Dodge, burn   46

SUPERPOSITION

Oracle   49
Self-Portrait as Pocket Watch   50
The Aesthetics of Disappearance   51
Any Day Now   53
Picture a Woman   54
Instructions for a Flightless Crow   56
Outlier   57
Year of Living Carefully   58
If, then   59
Her Wrists   60
Trompe-L'oeil   61
Anamorph along Highway 101   62
In the Church of Bric-a-Brac   63
Self-Portrait as Pomegranate   64
Afterword   66

Notes   69
Acknowledgments   72
About the Author   74

Entanglement

SELF-PORTRAIT AS BRUISE

A blood whisper,
I am the younger sister of impact,
the lost hour saving daylight mourns.

Mildew is my second cousin, once removed.
I'm often surreptitious, the small chameleon
on the back of a thigh or comma below the ear.

If there is a fresh pear on the counter,
I will press into it my yellow kiss.

I've been called reticent, understudy
to hostage and hospice, but I prefer to yell
when someone sees I'm there.

Thumbprint or thunderhead,
my longing will never be taken
for love, though it is similar

in the way it uses quiet fury
to aggravate intention
and pools with me in one place far too long.

DEADLOCK

Pre -

Under a tarnished sky, one moss-freighted limb
hunkers like a pathologist over the road to the lab

A Petri dish is tonged from its stack
A left breast, unpowdered, awaits its probe

The pet cat wandered off a week earlier,
climbed into a box at the neighbor's

Post -

The pathologist swivels her microscope
dice are in mid-roll, coin's in the air

Results = Pending

Crest and trough
holding heavy the simultaneous upshots

The marked breast is carried to bed,
patted down under the press of blankets

The old cat's dreamt alive

Regardless of outcome, every passage underneath
the laden maple will be a new snag in the chest

*Mrs. Schrödinger's breast is a playground
of mown paths studded with stones.
Children and lovers like to romp there.
It is also a graveyard, not in itself deadly
but where DNA is prone to rest.*

SQUARE ROOTS

the ability
to name the body of water
a particular wine
rises from

what happens
to the vine after grapes
are picked

the specific
seedling in a test-garden
to become a Stradivarius

recovering
the high-end fiddle
left in a taxi

for each optimist
there is a bright thing
traceable unsullied
back to its origin

then there is the pessimist
unruly guest at the table
who can't wait to hear
the back-story of carrion
before it meets the vulture's jaw

*Mrs. Schrödinger's breast ignores latitudes,
has no Greenwich Mean Time.
Cells inside exist three hours ago
or four hours ahead, depending
on velocity, pathology, expiration date.*

AT SALT CREEK FALLS

When hail,
raucous difficulty,
drops down

it pummels
in multitudes
and scuttles off
unscathed.

How to immunize
the precarious heart
from onslaught
and uninvited
aggravation?

Think swifts.

Solitary specks
of screaming frenzy
black
at the falls.

Stiff shallow
wing beats
in constant motion.

Cloud swifts.
Foragers of air.

To survive,
they must dive
through a megaton
veil, reach damp
nests behind
the waterfall.

Watch them
avoid predators
by not lingering.

MRS. SCHRÖDINGER TIES HER OWN FLIES

He's gone again.
Fishing his theorems
or reeling in the new student.
These entanglements . . .
How the slightest glitter attracts.

Were I as litigious as he is priapic
I might have taken him to court long ago.

Here's a gift of feathers: goose down
too elusive for the pillow.
I'll get the loupe from his desk,
tie a new fly from some fluff,
maybe stick one in his creel.

This time while he's away
I'll stop casting into the same dry lake.

Double-Slit Theory

SELF-PORTRAIT AS INSOMNIA

You know me.
Morpheus's busybody aunt.
I rattle around
setting quicksand
along the verges of night.
Disenfranchised from the land
of nod, no one blinks asleep
in my house.
No napping, no vampires
in their fragrant mahogany coffins,
no sweet baby
crescent eyes sealed shut
or lovers' post-coital
parched drowse.
I reprogram day for night
at random, render Ambien
useless as warm milk.
To be honest, though flattered
by rapt attention
from all my little midnight
monkey minds, I do weary
of the incessant push to entertain
& this diabolical graveyard shift.

FREEZE TAG

You
sidle
up
high school
reunion
fifty
years
since you
knew it all
anesthetized
leap of faith
childhood
sends
breathless
tilt-a-whirl
missives
step
forward
back

*Anny Schrödinger has adventures
in marital architecture with Erwin and Hilde.
She/they are jealous or not jealous.
An affair or no affair? Without seeing the lover as lover,
there is no possibility of betrayal.*

M & MS

He would arrive, random magazine under his arm, the bottle of champagne already oozing its tintinnabulation of bubbles, and present a crystal globe of bumblebees, or he'd dip behind her to clasp a necklace of diamond frogs set in platinum around her white neck, and announce the evening's outing—dinner in a Michelin three star or at the summer house of Duchess So and So. If she protested, if she asked if they could just once walk to the movies or do anything that didn't require an onyx-window'd limousine to transport them, he would scoff, treat her as so much phytoplankton until she came to her senses, until she resumed her role as snowgirl to his snowman. Eventually, he went on to someone else, as she knew he would. She could have killed him, but it seemed better to let the bad taste of him melt in her mouth, not in her hands.

*Mrs. Schrödinger's breast has needs: billboards
and a flash crowd to applaud beneath the balcony,
or sometimes, pendulous clouds
pranking virga to moisten new French lingerie
and undercut claustrophobia.*

SELF-PORTRAIT AS QUARREL

To begin, I am not a squall.
Don't call me that. Nor am I peckish,
under the weather or out of sorts.

You can find me anywhere.
I squint and have a guttered face,
stray whiskers, black seeds in my teeth.

I'm your ruffled feather,
overdue bills, expired prescriptions,
the relentless houseguest.

I'm the first pickle stuck
in the jar or the last ketchup plug
jamming the mouth of your bottle.

I'm the crystalized ice cream
left too long in the freezer,
cold tea in your cup too soon after pouring.

I abhor fact check or litmus test,
and I can stretch a point
like the best taffy in Atlantic City.

If we're to get along, do not slit open
a box with my good kitchen knife.
If you don't have anything nice
to say about someone, sit next to me.

DÉFENSE DE FUMER

They don't see the sign
No sparks are left either
No sizzling down
No ember *jamais*
They see nothing explicit
posted on the balconies
of all those high rise *gratte-ciels*

Their honeymoon year
the move to Paris
they both chain smoked
She'd straddle chairs backwards
& he would lean seductively
against door jambs tapping ash into his palm

They swore they could hear comets falling

On Bastille Day twelve summers later
she leans over packing boxes
an unlit Gauloise hanging from her lips

She underscores her maiden name with a marker
separates out her share of the *feux d'artifices*

The air conditioner ticks off
hours till sundown

WHEN A MERMAID COMES UNDONE

Inconsequential shells—sometimes a chipped agate—
pay them daily to the gods of hazard.

Stealth is your best suit
to unpucker those drenched lips.

Hide in reef shadow. Avoid
black-clad grief divers who grope after their own hearts.

If compromise swims by, as it will,
up-end that raft of innuendo and guilt.

Don't connive or flutter. Go deep.
If you let it, forgiveness will eventually save you.

*Mrs. Schrödinger's breast is not always hers.
There are thumbprints, nicknames: Oscar, Maribeth.
It might be a bullet in the chamber or a blank,
a lost key locked inside a room or not.
Perhaps it is a sandcastle rendered at high tide.*

DINNER AT THE *DÉJÀ VU*

If it's bad,
one of those colossal rows,
drive the freeway
downtown.
A litter patrol
will be stabbing
the shoulder
and traffic will creep
enough for buying
fresh artichokes
from a sun-cracked vendor
on the median.
If there is a feral woman
your age pacing
too close to the vendor,
try not to stare.
Just count your change.

It may or may not help
to recall Chicago.
December, 1972.
The glazed Eisenhower,
excessive speed.
Your ex, too proud
of his latest spin
for your protest.
He did reach across you
for the door handle.
He did shove.
You did find a new fire-
side to warm your cold feet.

Return home,
set the table.
Defrost a leftover
you loved the first time.
Boil water for a feral girl's
artichoke and one for your new spouse.
This is dinner at the *Déjà Vu*:
one set of teeth pulling fresh leaves
slowly for nourishment, another
going right to the choke.

HOW TO MAKE A VOODOO DOLL

Look in the mirror.

Name the target
but never say it aloud.

Take an insult,
say libel.

Or a bigger one:
failure of imagination.

Walk into the woods
until your pulse slows and breath returns.

While there, choose two sturdy twigs.
Lash them into a crucifix.

Wrap strangle-length ribbon, one inch wide,
wire-edged, around and around like a mummy.

Find crow feathers to stick on top,
then go rip three buttons from the target's shirt.

The buttons are eyes and mouth,
no need for a nose.

Begin at the crown, poke pins
all over the figure, spare no body part.

Carry around the punctured doll,
add or remove pins as you go.

Leave the doll alone
and return to your mirror. Stare.

If you made the doll correctly,
something is bound to change.

WORRY PEOPLE

In their thin oval wood box
the *muñecas quitapenas* are colorful and bent.
With arms in impossible angles,
the little dolls await
a new assignment before bed.

Unburdened of the last affair—
that fragrant reef of duplicity—
onto the *tapados* and *faldas* of the worry people,
the sleeper dreams of conch chowder,
darting parrotfish, a diver
in his sleek skin brushing her arm
at snorkel depth as he swims by.

Who wants to awaken this *soñadora*?
Every small lidded box in her house contains
something she's saved from a lost
encounter: sea urchin spine,
dental gold, eucalyptus pods, a fallen pearl.

If the trapped dolls can work it out
before daylight, let the pearl
and spine use the dark, too,
easing the pain
of a thousand other things that turn up.

*Anny Schrödinger occasionally feels like
a moose cow left behind, harrumphing
into thick grass. When that happens, she dreams
of purple ruched underwire demi push-ups,
structure and no-show petals.*

DECOHERENCE

MRS. SCHRÖDINGER'S MIRAGE OF CONVENIENCE

Constant, the shimmer
on desert roads in late summer.

Evanescent,

like that feeling
she recognizes what perches
on the high diving board
but she can't identify genus or species
or predict if she'll get drenched
from the splash.

SELF-PORTRAIT AS ROOTS

A dark house suits me.
I am where the raucous settles
between a tangle of fingers.
With *a salted methodology*
for drawing nutrients,
I'm a temptress of grubs,
storing essentials the ringed tenant
upstairs so dearly craves.
In my speakeasy, I'm free to ignore suitors
with their sawtooth blades.
Listen to me tap the old tunes *sotto voce*,
even when the music stops.

BELONGING

At first, one of anything marries the void.
One rattle, her voice. A hoop drum,
her heart.
Losing her,
sign and symbol seize
mute hours.

Flood

Bequests are the new lingua franca:
charm bracelet
ruby-clasped pearls
white kid gloves
navy blue rubber garden boots
the painted canvas bag to carry them.

Vestigial swell at the door
Her murky breath

Reprise

Any day now, my arms in her sweater,
when I think about waving, I'll see her.

PARTICLE OR WAVE

Before the house sale,
plucked from a dumpster,
an old suitcase, light tan with brown stripes,
holding a pocket watch, metal grooming kit
so shiny, the covered soap dish with curving sides
and a father's clothing
from the state hospital.
Empty of him is the khaki shirt
a sister, close to her own death, saved.

This sibling trip was for playing on the beach,
summoning boiled Maine lobsters, fireflies and cardinals,
and little-neck clams from Rosie's on Route 4.

What's left from their past trips
is a vestigial father, splintery with speculation.
And from this one, a photo:
two sisters holding on to each other
in the surf up to their knees.

ONE DOES NOT TELL THE FUTURE   IT TELLS US

> after a line from Allan Peterson

One does not tell a sister
when she does not ask for help
that you are helpless.

One cannot imagine the number
of rooms the housekeeper must sweep
in the house of grief.

If spring blares magnolia and forsythia
too soon, relax. There is no practical way
to quash them.

What does one give a sister
in the numbed hours
before the future arrives?

Perhaps something simple
from childhood.
Like a new roll of Life Savers
and the offer for her to
choose all her colors first.

HOW THE TEMPORARY BECOMES PERMANENT

In the time it takes a flipped penny
to land on the back of a freckled hand
most would turn past a news story
of the state hospital's unclaimed remains.

Row upon row of copper urns—
ten across, nine high—draw me
in among the scalloped shadows
under each canister, each gleam
and stripe of fluorescent light.

My father's Westclox Pocket Ben
ticks off the years since he disappeared
into madness. I taste the metallic bite,
wish I could straighten his tortoise-rimmed glasses,
loosen the clench of his oversize hands.

Supermarket of the out of bounds,
this "room of unknown souls."
The urns are like Crosse & Blackwell consommé
stored in the family cellar
where metal corrodes just short of bursting.

WHAT DOES NOT REQUIRE WINGS

That spring, oldest sister   your last smoke rings   Perfumed circles rise

Hiking the Canyon del Muerto   I pry agates from the trail

As kids   our dad absent   two imaginary horses play all day

Here's your fox fetish   laced with medicine

Canyon horses watch   Our Navajo guide chants up the prudent granaries

At summer camp   sugar cubes clenched in our hands

        you *owned* that palomino Goldie

17-year cicadas return   red eyes burn through cacophony

        Rings of smoke   a sibling's corral   gives way

MIRAGE

Your brain has escaped
its bone house

Stories shimmer
like soldiers floating
on Gulf War roads

This grey matter
panned for gold
words grooving eight decades
now silenced
in memory care

Every day you wait
for your long-dead brother
He might be the God particle
or a white bucket turned egret
invisible to everyone but you

Or he might be someone's
missing breast
still needing to be caressed
reclaiming the void
in its yearning

SCANT MEASURE

Dry-eyed, she is silent at his vault.
Nothing left to say or sift
yet every condolence left beside the bridge

deepens her color, her need to bridge
a span of one dusk, vault
from companion to widow who sifts

her hair for sea wrack, asks strangers to sift
the last of him, ebony-boxed, from under a bridge.
A handkerchief clumsy in her hand against the vault.

Will this vault, his residue of sift, allow her a full cup, or scant life,
                                                                                  abridged?

SEVENTH SIDE OF THE DIE

    a found poem

In the middle of this poised assembly
shafts of afternoon light filter through
an elevated dream of perfection.

Swines in the terroir of prayerful sogginess
say *to sing is to be loved*
and a vast array of protector deities

may be called upon to stay
the dormancy which makes it
all that much sadder.

All my life amphibious memory's
perpetually altering the ruins
of chairs and escalators.

When you need cold as much as others
need warmth you hold on
to the smallest marvel of appeasement.

INSTRUCTIONS FOR A FIRST-TIME WIDOW

Remember,
you are no caretaker of air.
Keep your mouth open
like a bronze goddess
who maintains reciprocal stillness.

Keep company with spiders
and elephants, those sweet
preposterous scouts,
for they know the way back
from bruxing rivers and gridlock.

When you feel naïve
let a memory slide up
through your kelp hands.
Be the green slug bride
trailing a viscous train.

Do not be the extinct Basilosaurus,
or Hell's Canyon swallowing
its own weather.
Snap to, now. There's no air raid drill
in your town this year.

Get out from under that tiny desk.
Hear the first brash frog of spring.

HER TREASURED EXTRAVAGANCE

       a cento, from and for H.J.W.

          i
If any tree is ever ours except to care for
we become each other's stories
knowing it might never be enough

          ii
In just this way life keeps sending me decoys:
It's a slow spiraling
It takes a patience past comparing
Nothing ever lies too deep to erupt

          iii
For a slivered moment, she senses her old self
her every step must be won over expectation
she would plant her low consolation
to nourish and heal with a strength beyond its reach

          iv
sometimes skin deep is deep enough
but who can live on the quivering end of joy?
Home, I celebrate the small—

Field Theory

WHEN DEMONS BLINK

> after *Basin #13* ~ a work on paper by Robert Tomlinson

Inside a metropolis of stars
lurks no force able to spring
elders from their grave vigils

They watch traceries of longing
trail asteroid mayhem
emblematic of each incandescent conundrum

A screech-silent sky
pops open beyond the brink

Life-straw and torch,
memory, pantomime—they try everything
to escape verticality or vermicular fates

even as their unruly DNA
stays in discrete columns unmoved
by pivot, the sweet enticement of astral twist

ON THE VERGE

      a hornet hung-

over from summer
in a rubber boot

        comes to life

dormant hornet
low-flying hornet
Lazarus hornet

          rises
                circles

elapsed time on its back

does it want out
      or

has it dreamt enough
chambered vocation to last

        another season

ANNY'S CONUNDRUM

Was it *folie à deux*
or *trois* that allowed me
to share Erwin with Hilde
all these years?
No man is an island.
But some are peninsulas
around which the waters
can't help but lap.

MY AVOCADO, THIS CHEEKY ADDICTION

You think you are so hot,
Triumph-green perched
atop the mound.
I've been there.

You start off beautiful—
taut, firm like your eggplant friend.
But any passerby can see
the propensity to bruise.

Like me, thin-skinned, flesh-challenged
and with absinthe breath,
you won't last an hour in open air.
Your epicenter's one hard knot.

Yet, I continue to fall for you
and all that green hype.
Fingers splayed, I must caress your flaunted virtue
as your divine curvature masks the slump.

Anny's breast is a ferry carrying sex between eye and groin. All hands on deck *becomes a gull cry released from her voluminous brig.*

DODGE, BURN

For the right exposure
shoot the gnarl,
tinker a light whirl.
Between subject and desired effect
shine extra moon.

In the warm pillowcase,
a clogged waterfall.

To adjust the cumbrous
press of [   ] *doubt*?
there's a caffeine mountain,
some owls dopplering.
And geese dusky, geese white.

Darkening the new page:
black lines—a bird abacus—
waiting for sun to count wings,
to burn through.

SUPERPOSITION

ORACLE

after Woman with Pomegranates by Bill Rane

Airborne, the seeds of desire
        my juicy ones   my girls
   three universes in my lap.

This one, so plump and extravagant,
      her secrets   ready
to slip down a suitor's chin.

That one will spill   girls
   until a boy shoulders through.

And this, my last darling
                with dry breath astounding,

    will shrivel, but not too soon

and perch on the table   re-seeding a recalcitrant muse.

On my wedding night:
              pomegranates

   placed on the doorstep by well-meaning maids.

I called to them:

          Come, juggle chance
          till dawn's rose.
          Take three, leave three
          and set one out for the gods to toss
          in their indiscriminate play.

My dearests,   O womb-webbed joy—
      Sluice,
              drip the forty years.

Dry and fluff your sheets.
            Slice,

replenish.

        One seed is all it takes.

SELF-PORTRAIT AS POCKET WATCH

Timeless when lying at rest,
I am noncommittal's ore.
Wind me and around I go,
each point on my face significant and vital.

With spider thread I sweep and stretch,
overlap night with day. My heart
ticks in perfect rhythm, slowly, deliberately.
My second hand is, strictly speaking, a third.

From first degree to last, I am small, but truthful.
He or she who holds me can stop me cold
or release the power to start a race, catch planes,
detonate bombs, pinpoint birth or death.

I do not veer or wobble depending on the news.
I am my own statistician.
Call me simple, analog, old-fashioned, punctual.
Momentum is nothing to me.

In fact, I've retired, but still hold a single job:
telling time forward and back to a woman
whose long-missing father warmed me in his hand.
She curls me in hers, steadfastly drawn to my heat.

THE AESTHETICS OF DISAPPEARANCE

It seems barely a minute since winter raged and being snowed in got old. Two weeks after the solstice and the extra light is perceivable on magnolia buds shy in their calyxes at five o'clock. What if the turmoil in your girl could belay down a mogul'd wall and walk to the park as easily. One day she'd be lifting her palm or a chair to confront, the next, when the only thing different was that light shone on the back of her head as it hadn't for weeks, she'd soften, raise her chin as if charged by a photovoltaic cell. On December's bleakest afternoon, or when tire chains trigger a migraine, do you recall how early the white hellebores bloom? Those drooping heads are not fragile or despondent. They thrive, like DNA, and persist in a realm between darkest and dark.

*Mrs. Schrödinger's breast has no standard cup size.
Is the cup half full or half empty?
Handful or sweaterful, a fitting gauge?
To measure or contain is an insult
if volume is ever to be increased or diminished.*

ANY DAY NOW

A door stutters open.
You've turned all the tables,
rearranged furniture.
Your telephone, coffee pot, forks, spoons,
once familiar, are now cluttered banter
shearing hinges off cupboards.
Snickering windows
collect the rickety.
Shutters are halcyon
inexplicable tickets to impinge on dust.
The tea water is boiling.
Will you sit or stand?

PICTURE A WOMAN

in her youth who feigned
muteness to neighborhood taunters
and lied to a mugger's knife.

She was mute. She was not mute
to the bullies only if they heard her speak.
Her wallet held cash
only if one of them looked inside.

*Mrs. Schrödinger doesn't travel much.
When she does, it's Turkish baths, Irish tombs,
leaning into birdbaths and holy water fonts.
Everywhere signposts awaken memories
of hands curved to warm her.*

INSTRUCTIONS FOR A FLIGHTLESS CROW

     for Fatema

To see better
affix a sable blindfold

To inhale enough sound
recall the frightened skunk

Do not swallow your own flag
to launch the fierce protest

Never faint if hoodwinking prey is your goal
Gnaw from the snake's opposite end

Believe each rising thermal
is strapped to your tree of a heart

You may still kick free
from the blackest of edens

There is little to be done
about your broken wing

OUTLIER

In a year when depth hoar
raises avalanche risk
there is a frequent wanderer,
a woman who never took up skis.

No skis, but if offered shelter she maintains
a collection of clattering white plates—
armor to fend off purgatory
or niggling obsessions.

Not wax paper obsessions, but real
situations involving bats hugging
the windows, a sore toe, slugs on the counter,
a small rabbit in the tub.

In a tub, she is Vasco da Gama
exploring heel, ankle, mole, rash, cyst
until a window of discovery opens
and she can slip out of her plague of skin.

She will not learn how to ski,
nor will she cause a single avalanche.
Don't mind her. She is more content
than most navigating the opaque.

Inside or outside her skin any conversation
she has with the finite is tentative.

YEAR OF LIVING CAREFULLY

Stared
almost
could
not find
Jupiter
looking
was
worthless
compared to
imagining
your winged heart
roaming
night
catching
the random
updraft
soul
trying
flight

IF, THEN

She would turn her house inside out
for you if you visited, finding a pin
to put in the exact town on the map of you.

She lives everywhere and nowhere
or where you live.
She wears her sleeping bag
so she can always be in her own bed.

Her tea leaves mix with yours,
your toothbrushes lock bristles
on the edge of the sink.
Your headaches are her poems.

If you are a waterfall, she is the rock
over which you spill. If you are the rock,
she's magma, still rising.

HER WRISTS

are glass, Pyrex, tempered
by tapping on church doors.

Her mission: Brinks trucks toting
immutable sparks of treasure fresh off the pyre.

She tucks unmet needs
into glassine envelopes,

lets one seed at a time spill
from a torn corner.

She bloats the flash of circumstance
to bleed blink pop breed.

A Manhattan, all fists,
she could be the New Year's baby, fired up,

refracting too much noise and light
when the Waterford ball drops.

TROMPE-L'OEIL

cartoon bomblets on a kitchen floor
popped corn escapes the pan

outdoors, DayGlo gutter-flung
clumps of moss splotch the lawn

same kitchen, four kittens nurse—
their mouths little hinges at a nipple

curbside, the brindled yellow dog splayed
across the sidewalk is in fact a cardboard box

in a downtown garage, Parking Level B
kitten-size clusters dot the crazed ramp

corn will tremble to life in seconds
moss and cats' heads will fill
a palm with equal precision

does any of this sound familiar
stranded popcorn, gutter moss, abandoned kittens
before or after, are you the one who gathers them up

ANAMORPH ALONG HIGHWAY 101

October downpour
The bicyclist rides his lane
backpack screen-printed with a skull

Holbein's *Ambassadors* in your mind

Whether you have the right braking distance
or a device on hand to view it
the skull appears

That slant, the caught moment
slicing cold rain

IN THE CHURCH OF BRIC-A-BRAC

& crimp
you find me confessing
stirring each naughty
round & round
steeping my least warp

you find a menial windmill
flipping the truth
batting & batting
until it's bereft of initiative

you hasten to chasten
me on my high escalator
where it is too easy to wait
& wait till the last second
to step off

how frustrating that windmill
& the escalator
it keeps rising & rising
only to fall

SELF-PORTRAIT AS POMEGRANATE

Forget that old myth, tough as dried fruit.
Open your mind and you'll come
to me with more respect.
I am doyenne of the table, of the cupped hand,
the orbed depression in stone.
Not everyone bursts murder into a room with one cut
or holds secrets like rubies under a dimpled coat.
A Chinese finger puzzle, entrapment, I am not.
I open, heedless of consequences. Think what can happen
to tires at an exit, all the small lacerations from backing up,
from forgetting the thing you came for.

The way into me is deceptively simple.
Out can be messy, but sweet is the stain
that keeps repeating its tale.

If your breast is natal-flat, can it be roused?
Even if your chest is scraped to the bone
like a butte lowered by truckloads
might you still hear winter wren-song,
that spirited trill and chatter?

AFTERWORD

unfinished letter from the author to Annemarie Bertel Schrödinger

Dear Anny,

This comes to you from decades
beyond your life-span, but following
my recent biopsy and the briefest
acquaintance with your husband's
experiments in quantum physics,
I thought you more than anyone
would understand how I fell
into total decoherence
during that infernal waiting period
between the test and its results.
Maybe after you read this letter and
some other bits I've put together here,
you could send a signal (a wave, perhaps?)
to keep me from collapsing
into the confounding state of predictability.

There isn't a large backstory
for you to absorb. My life has
been fairly normal to this point—
less complicated than yours. I've had two husbands,
but not at the same time. Some lovers, but
pardon me, no musical chairs or managing
all that sheet changing you and Erwin
must have done. Like you, no biological children,
though stepchildren are intricately woven
into my life as I suppose Ruth was in yours.
Did you know that a crater on the far side
of the moon was named for Erwin?
Sorry, I digress.

Back to the biopsy, so I won't keep you
suspended for too long.
Going blindly into the procedure was helpful
and the test itself was nothing.
It was the wait for results, as I said earlier,
that slayed me. Those moments
when I had cancer and did not have cancer

simultaneously were when I began to think
of my breast as cousin to your breast
and perhaps interspecies cousin
to Erwin's famous cat inside its box.
Until someone *observed* my cells
and reported back to me,
I was suspended in hapless limbo.

As time passed, I started talking to my breasts,
addressing them as if they were sentient beings.
Was I losing my mind? Did that ever happen to you
when your breasts were now in Erwin's
now in Arthur's or Weyl's hands?
It was easier to let my breasts imagine yours
(please excuse my liberties with your anatomy)
than carve a groove in the floor from anxiety.

So, Anny, I wish you were still alive.
Since I have not personally seen you dead,
perhaps you are as alive as I envision my father is.
(He went missing in 1968. But that is another story.)
If I have trespassed on your reputation,
forgive me. I will hope for plenty

NOTES

Erwin Rudolf Josef Alexander Schrödinger (1887-1961) was an Austrian physicist renowned for his work in quantum physics, wave mechanics (for which he won the Nobel Prize in 1933), optics, thermodynamics, unified field theory, and a host of other scientific disciplines. His path from birth in Vienna and back there led him to teach widely in Europe and at Dublin's Institute for Advanced Studies. His books include scientific studies and personal philosophy.

His famous thought experiment, known as "Schrödinger's Cat," was devised in 1935 to challenge a certain interpretation of quantum mechanics: superposition of states and when the states are said to collapse into one. The experiment, also described as a paradox, goes like this: A cat is placed in a box rigged inside with a vial of poison, a small deadly radioactive source, and a radiation detector. If the detector detects radiation, the vial breaks and its poison kills the cat. If no radiation is detected, the poison is withheld and the cat remains alive. Until the box is opened and the cat is observed alive *or* dead, theoreticians posited the cat could be assumed alive and dead *simultaneously*. Erwin set out to discuss the paradox of two opposing simultaneous states of matter and the absurdity of such an interpretation. It is the play with this simultaneity of states, absurd as they may be, that intrigues the author of this collection.

Erwin was married to Annemarie (Anny) Bertel (1896-1965). Anny was born in Salzburg, Austria. Her father was a court photographer, the family prosperous. She and Erwin had a long, colorful open marriage. Erwin, with no children by Anny, had many lovers, including several of his students (who bore him children) and the wife of his assistant, Arthur March. Hilde March gave birth to Erwin's daughter and moved in with the Schrödingers as 'second wife' to raise the child. Anny was Arthur's lover and then Hermann Weyl's. Anny's story has more to it and slips under Erwin's. [See Walter J. Moore's *Schrödinger: Life and Thought* for a thorough account of Erwin's work and his and Anny's personal escapades.]

The headings separating sections are ordinarily the vocabulary of physics. In this collection, the author allows the terms to range 'outside the box,' and hopes the integrity of the terms themselves will echo among the poems.

Entanglement	A state where an observer becomes 'entangled' with an object, e.g. with the live or dead cat in Erwin Schrödinger's thought experiment.
Double-Slit Theory	Describes situations in which matter and energy can display characteristics of both wave and particle.
Decoherence	Describes experimental outcomes that have no interaction with each other.
Field Theory	A theory explaining physical phenomena in terms of a particular field and how it interacts with matter or with other fields; a state with infinite degrees of freedom.
Superposition	Describes a *mixture* of states until they collapse into a single state. (Again, the cat both alive and dead simultaneously until one or the other state is observed.)

"Any Day Now." *16th International Congress of World Art* (2009): Print.

"Belonging" is for HQB.

"Her Treasured Extravagance." Cento from Hannah Wilson (1928-2004). The title and lines in this poem are sourced from Hannah's poems as follows: "The Timbre of Her Voice," "If Any Tree is Ever Ours," "Doubling," "Earthquake," "At the Post Office," "Transformation," "Late Summer in the Garden," "Coast Starlight," "In Rehab," "Second Child," "Clea," "Garlic Braiding," "Balm," "Prodigal Chair" and "Gleanings."

"*One does not tell the future   it tells us*" is the first line in "Frequent Flyer" by Allan Peterson. This poem is for LHB.

"Oracle" was exhibited as a broadside in the ekphrastic exhibition featuring Bill Rane paintings at the Rane Gallery, Taos, New Mexico, 2009.

"Scant Measure" is a tritina.

"Self-Portrait as Roots." The phrase 'a salted methodology' is quoted from Cecily Parks, "Self-Portrait Which Makes Use of the Beaufort Scale" *Field Folly Snow*.

"Seventh Side of the Die." The lines are sourced from *The Economist*, *Financial Times* and *The New Yorker*.

"What Does Not Require Wings" is for SHS.

"Year of Living Carefully" is for David Johnson (1945-2006).

"Year of Living Carefully" and "Freeze Tag" are 'waltz waves,' a syllabic form.

ACKNOWLEDGMENTS

Thanks to the editors of the following journals and books in which these poems first appeared:

"Her Wrists" and *"Défense de Fumer." Turn.* Ed. Laura LeHew. Eugene, OR: Uttered Chaos, 2013. Print.

"If, then" and "How the Temporary Becomes Permanent." *Refuge from Flux.* Georgetown, KY: Finishing Line, 2010. Print.

"Instructions for a First-Time Widow." *Lakeview International Journal of Literature and Arts.* Delhi, India: Forthcoming.

"Instructions for a Flightless Crow." *Noctua Review.* Vol. 6, 2013. Print.

"Mirage." *Ayris Magazine.* 2013. Print.

"Particle or Wave" and "What Does Not Require Wings." *The Knotted Bond: Oregon Poets Speak of Their Sisters.* Ed. Liz Nakazawa. Eugene, OR: Uttered Chaos, 2014. Print.

"Scant Measure" and "Dodge, burn." *The Medulla Review.* Vol. 2, No. 1, 2010. Web.

"Self-Portrait as Bruise." *Paper Nautilus.* 2013. Print.

"When Demons Blink." *Original Weather: A Collection of Art and Poems.* Ed. Laura LeHew. Eugene, OR: Uttered Chaos, 2011. Print.

"Worry People." *Collecting Life: Poets on Objects Known and Imagined.* Ed. Madelyn Garner and Andrea L. Watson. Denver, CO: 3: A Taos, 2011. Print.

To faithful members of Kwinnim and 1st & 3rd Poets, and those who have taken time with some of these poems, robust thanks for your thoughtful critiques which help guide words to their true north.

My appreciation and deep thanks to Judy Montgomery for years of mentoring and monitoring my work. And thanks to Allan Peterson and Penelope Scambly Schott. Each of you fosters and enhances my life in poetry.

Immense gratitude to Nancy Carol Moody for engagement and candor with all stages of this book. I am enriched by the countless instances of her keenest eye, depth of insight, and her kind heart keeping me on track within and beyond the pages here.

A hundred-flag salute to my indefatigable friend, editor, and publisher, Laura LeHew. Her support of this poet and others and her active involvement in broadening access to Oregon poets through her press, salons, workshops, and critique groups is epic. I'm honored to be part of Uttered Chaos and to unfurl these poems under Laura's wing.

And for Dennis Gould, I am staggeringly grateful.

ABOUT THE AUTHOR

Quinton Hallett writes and edits from her rural property in Noti, Oregon. She is the author of three chapbooks, founder of Fern Rock Falls Press, and her work appears or is forthcoming in journals and anthologies including: *Windfall, Ayris, Tiger's Eye, Paper Nautilus, Cirque, The Knotted Bond, Till the Tide,* and *december*. She has coordinated a reading series and high school poet visits for the Oregon Poetry Association, and received residencies from Caldera and Soapstone. She reads a selection of poems on the Oregon Poetic Voices website (oregonpoeticvoices.org). In 2013, an animated short film by John Haugse featured one of her poems, "To the Long Ago Maybes." In a previous incarnation, Quinton organized exhibitions for the Smithsonian Institution Traveling Exhibition Service (SITES) and the Armand Hammer Foundation in Los Angeles.

www.ingramcontent.com/pod-product-compliance
Lightning Source LLC
Chambersburg PA
CBHW032210040426
42449CB00005B/526